Key Judgments

Iraq's Weapons of Mass Destruction Programs

Iraq has continued its weapons of mass destruction (WMD) programs in defiance of UN resolutions and restrictions. Baghdad has chemical and biological weapons as well as missiles with ranges in excess of UN restrictions; if left unchecked, it probably will have a nuclear weapon during this decade.

Baghdad hides large portions of Iraq's WMD efforts. Revelations after the Gulf war starkly demonstrate the extensive efforts undertaken by Iraq to deny information.

Since inspections ended in 1998, Iraq has maintained its chemical weapons effort, energized its missile program, and invested more heavily in biological weapons; most analysts assess Iraq is reconstituting its nuclear weapons program.

- Iraq's growing ability to sell oil illicitly increases Baghdad's capabilities to finance WMD programs; annual earnings in cash and goods have more than quadrupled.

- Iraq largely has rebuilt missile and biological weapons facilities damaged during Operation Desert Fox and has expanded its chemical and biological infrastructure under the cover of civilian production.

- Baghdad has exceeded UN range limits of 150 km with its ballistic missiles and is working with unmanned aerial vehicles (UAVs), which allow for a more lethal means to deliver biological and, less likely, chemical warfare agents.

- Although Saddam probably does not yet have nuclear weapons or sufficient material to make any, he remains intent on acquiring them.

How quickly Iraq will obtain its first nuclear weapon depends on when it acquires sufficient weapons-grade fissile material.

- If Baghdad acquires sufficient weapons-grade fissile material from abroad, it could make a nuclear weapon within a year.

- Without such material from abroad, Iraq probably would not be able to make a weapon until the last half of the decade.

  — Iraq's aggressive attempts to obtain proscribed high-strength aluminum tubes are of significant concern. All intelligence experts agree that Iraq is seeking nuclear weapons and that these tubes could be used in a centrifuge enrichment program. Most intelligence specialists assess this to be the intended use, but some believe that these tubes are probably intended for conventional weapons programs.

— Based on tubes of the size Iraq is trying to acquire, a few tens of thousands of centrifuges would be capable of producing enough highly enriched uranium for a couple of weapons per year.

Baghdad has begun renewed production of chemical warfare agents, probably including mustard, sarin, cyclosarin, and VX. Its capability was reduced during the UNSCOM inspections and is probably more limited now than it was at the time of the Gulf war, although VX production and agent storage life probably have been improved.

- Saddam probably has stocked a few hundred metric tons of CW agents.

- The Iraqis have experience in manufacturing CW bombs, artillery rockets, and projectiles, and probably possess CW bulk fills for SRBM warheads, including for a limited number of covertly stored, extended-range Scuds.

All key aspects—R&D, production, and weaponization—of Iraq's offensive BW program are active and most elements are larger and more advanced than they were before the Gulf wa r.

- Iraq has some lethal and incapacitating BW agents and is capable of quickly producing and weaponizing a variety of such agents, including anthrax, for delivery by bombs, missiles, aerial sprayers, and covert operatives, including potentially against the US Homeland.

- Baghdad has established a large-scale, redundant, and concealed BW agent production capability, which includes mobile facilities; these facilities can evade detection, are highly survivable, and can exceed the production rates Iraq had prior to the Gulf war.

Iraq maintains a small missile force and several development programs, including for a UAV that most analysts believe probably is intended to deliver biological warfare agents.

- Gaps in Iraqi accounting to UNSCOM suggest that Saddam retains a covert force of up to a few dozen Scud-variant SRBMs with ranges of 650 to 900 km.

- Iraq is deploying its new al-Samoud and Ababil-100 SRBMs, which are capable of flying beyond the UN-authorized 150-km range limit.

- Baghdad's UAVs—especially if used for delivery of chemical and biological warfare (CBW) agents—could threaten Iraq's neighbors, US forces in the Persian Gulf, and the United States if brought close to, or into, the US Homeland.

- Iraq is developing medium-range ballistic missile capabilities, largely through foreign assistance in building specialized facilities.

Discussion

Iraq's Weapons of Mass Destruction Programs

In April 1991, the UN Security Council enacted Resolution 687 requiring Iraq to declare, destroy, or render harmless its weapons of mass destruction (WMD) arsenal and production infrastructure under UN or International Atomic Energy Agency (IAEA) supervision. UN Security Council Resolution (UNSCR) 687 also demanded that Iraq forgo the future development or acquisition of WMD.

Baghdad's determination to hold onto a sizeable remnant of its WMD arsenal, agents, equipment, and expertise has led to years of dissembling and obstruction of UN inspections. Elite Iraqi security services orchestrated an extensive concealment and deception campaign to hide incriminating documents and material that precluded resolution of key issues pertaining to its WMD programs.

- Iraqi obstructions prompted the Security Council to pass several subsequent resolutions demanding that Baghdad comply with its obligations to cooperate with the inspection process and to provide United Nations Special Commission (UNSCOM) and IAEA officials immediate and unrestricted access to any site they wished to inspect.

- Although outwardly maintaining the facade of cooperation, Iraqi officials frequently denied or substantially delayed access to facilities, personnel, and documents in an effort to conceal critical information about Iraq's WMD programs.

Successive Iraqi declarations on Baghdad's pre-Gulf war WMD programs gradually became more accurate between 1991 and 1998, but only because of sustained pressure from UN sanctions, Coalition military force, and vigorous and robust inspections facilitated by information from cooperative countries. Nevertheless, **Iraq never has fully accounted for major gaps and inconsistencies in its declarations and has provided no credible proof that it has completely destroyed its weapons stockpiles and production infrastructure**.

- UNSCOM inspection activities and Coalition military strikes destroyed most of its prohibited ballistic missiles and some Gulf war-era chemical and biological munitions, but Iraq still has a small force of extended-range Scud-variant missiles, chemical precursors, biological seed stock, and thousands of munitions suitable for chemical and biological agents.

- Iraq has preserved and in some cases enhanced the infrastructure and expertise necessary for WMD production and has used that capability to maintain a stockpile of WMD and to increase its size and sophistication in some areas.

UN Security Council Resolutions and Provisions for Inspections and Monitoring: Theory and Practice

Resolution Requirement	Reality
Res. 687 (3 April 1991) Requires Iraq to declare, destroy, remove, or render harmless under UN or IAEA supervision and not to use, develop, construct, or acquire all chemical and biological weapons, all ballistic missiles with ranges greater than 150 km, and all nuclear weapons-usable material, including related material, equipment, and facilities. The resolution also formed the Special Commission and authorized the IAEA to carry out immediate on-site inspections of WMD-related facilities based on Iraq's declarations and UNSCOM's designation of any additional locations.	Baghdad refused to declare all parts of each WMD program, submitted several declarations as part of its aggressive efforts to deny and deceive inspectors, and ensured that certain elements of the program would remain concealed. The prohibition against developing delivery platforms with ranges greater than 150 km allowed Baghdad to research and develop shorter-range systems with applications for longer-range systems and did not affect Iraqi efforts to convert full-size aircraft into unmanned aerial vehicles as potential WMD delivery systems with ranges far beyond 150 km.
Res. 707 (15 August 1991) Requires Iraq to allow UN and IAEA inspectors immediate and unrestricted access to any site they wish to inspect. Demands Iraq provide full, final, and complete disclosure of all aspects of its WMD programs; cease immediately any attempt to conceal, move, or destroy WMD-related material or equipment; allow UNSCOM and IAEA teams to use fixed-wing and helicopter flights throughout Iraq; and respond fully, completely, and promptly to any Special Commission questions or requests.	Baghdad in 1996 negotiated with UNSCOM Executive Chairman Ekeus modalities that it used to delay inspections, to restrict to four the number of inspectors allowed into any site Baghdad declared as "sensitive," and to prohibit them altogether from sites regarded as sovereign. These modalities gave Iraq leverage over individual inspections. Iraq eventually allowed larger numbers of inspectors into such sites but only after lengthy negotiations at each site.
Res. 715 (11 October 1991) Requires Iraq to submit to UNSCOM and IAEA long-term monitoring of Iraqi WMD programs; approved detailed plans called for in UNSCRs 687 and 707 for long-term monitoring.	Iraq generally accommodated UN monitors at declared sites but occasionally obstructed access and manipulated monitoring cameras. UNSCOM and IAEA monitoring of Iraq's WMD programs does not have a specified end date under current UN resolutions.
Res. 1051 (27 March 1996) Established the Iraqi export/import monitoring system, requiring UN members to provide IAEA and UNSCOM with information on materials exported to Iraq that may be applicable to WMD production, and requiring Iraq to report imports of all dual-use items.	Iraq is negotiating contracts for procuring—outside of UN controls—dual-use items with WMD applications. The UN lacks the staff needed to conduct thorough inspections of goods at Iraq's borders and to monitor imports inside Iraq.
Res. 1060 (12 June 1996) and Resolutions 1115, 1134, 1137, 1154, 1194, and 1205. Demands that Iraq cooperate with UNSCOM and allow inspection teams immediate, unconditional, and unrestricted access to facilities for inspection and access to Iraqi officials for interviews. UNSCR 1137 condemns Baghdad's refusal to allow entry to Iraq to UNSCOM officials on the grounds of their nationality and its threats to the safety of UN reconnaissance aircraft.	Baghdad consistently sought to impede and limit UNSCOM's mission in Iraq by blocking access to numerous facilities throughout the inspection process, often sanitizing sites before the arrival of inspectors and routinely attempting to deny inspectors access to requested sites and individuals. At times, Baghdad would promise compliance to avoid consequences, only to renege later.
Res. 1154 (2 March 1998) Demands that Iraq comply with UNSCOM and IAEA inspections and endorses the Secretary General's memorandum of understanding with Iraq, providing for "severest consequences" if Iraq fails to comply. **Res. 1194 (9 September 1998)** Condemns Iraq's decision to suspend cooperation with UNSCOM and the IAEA. **Res. 1205 (5 November 1998)** Condemns Iraq's decision to cease cooperation with UNSCOM.	UNSCOM could not exercise its mandate without Iraqi compliance. Baghdad refused to work with UNSCOM and instead negotiated with the Secretary General, whom it believed would be more sympathetic to Iraq's needs.
Res. 1284 (17 December 1999) Established the United Nations Monitoring, Verification, and Inspection Commission (UNMOVIC), replacing UNSCOM; and demanded that Iraq allow UNMOVIC teams immediate, unconditional, and unrestricted access to any and all aspects of Iraq's WMD program.	Iraq repeatedly has rejected the return of UN arms inspectors and claims that it has satisfied all UN resolutions relevant to disarmament. Compared with UNSCOM, 1284 gives the UNMOVIC chairman less authority, gives the Security Council a greater role in defining key disarmament tasks, and requires that inspectors be full-time UN employees.

Since December 1998, Baghdad has refused to allow UN inspectors into Iraq as required by the Security Council resolutions. Technical monitoring systems installed by the UN at known and suspected WMD and missile facilities in Iraq no longer operate. Baghdad prohibits Security Council-mandated monitoring overflights of Iraqi facilities by UN aircraft and helicopters. Similarly, Iraq has curtailed most IAEA inspections since 1998, allowing the IAEA to visit annually only a very small number of sites to safeguard Iraq's stockpile of uranium oxide.

In the absence of inspectors, Baghdad's already considerable ability to work on prohibited programs without risk of discovery has increased, and there is substantial evidence that Iraq is reconstituting prohibited programs. Baghdad's vigorous concealment efforts have meant that specific information on many aspects of Iraq's WMD programs is yet to be uncovered. Revelations after the Gulf war starkly demonstrate the extensive efforts undertaken by Iraq to deny information.

- Limited insight into activities since 1998 clearly show that Baghdad has used the absence of UN inspectors to repair and expand dual-use and dedicated missile-development facilities and to increase its ability to produce WMD.

Nuclear Weapons Program

More than ten years of sanctions and the loss of much of Iraq's physical nuclear infrastructure under IAEA oversight have not diminished Saddam's interest in acquiring or developing nuclear weapons.

- Iraq's efforts to procure tens of thousands of proscribed high-strength aluminum tubes are of significant concern. All intelligence experts agree that Iraq is seeking nuclear weapons and that these tubes could be used in a centrifuge enrichment program. Most intelligence specialists assess this to be the intended use, but some believe that these tubes are probably intended for conventional weapons programs.

Iraq had an advanced nuclear weapons development program before the Gulf war that focused on building an implosion-type weapon using highly enriched uranium. Baghdad was attempting a variety of uranium enrichment techniques, the most successful of which were the electromagnetic isotope separation (EMIS) and gas centrifuge programs. After its invasion of Kuwait, Iraq initiated a crash program to divert IAEA-safeguarded, highly enriched uranium from its Soviet and French-supplied reactors, but the onset of hostilities ended this effort. Iraqi declarations and the UNSCOM/IAEA inspection process revealed much of Iraq's nuclear weapons efforts, but Baghdad still has not provided complete information on all aspects of its nuclear weapons program.

- Iraq has withheld important details relevant to its nuclear program, including procurement logs, technical documents, experimental data, accounting of materials, and foreign assistance.

- Baghdad also continues to withhold other data about enrichment techniques, foreign procurement, weapons design, and the role of Iraqi security services in concealing its nuclear facilities and activities.

- In recent years, Baghdad has diverted goods contracted under the Oil-for-Food Program for military purposes and has increased solicitations and dual-use procurements—outside the Oil-for-Food process—some of which almost certainly are going to prohibited WMD and other weapons programs. Baghdad probably uses some of the money it gains through its illicit oil sales to support its WMD efforts.

Before its departure from Iraq, the IAEA made significant strides toward dismantling Iraq's nuclear weapons program and unearthing the nature and scope of Iraq's past nuclear activities. In the absence of inspections, however, most analysts assess that Iraq is reconstituting its nuclear program—unraveling the IAEA's hard-earned accomplishments.

Iraq retains its cadre of nuclear scientists and technicians, its program documentation, and sufficient dual-use manufacturing capabilities to support a reconstituted nuclear weapons program. Iraqi media have reported numerous meetings between Saddam and nuclear scientists over the past two years, signaling Baghdad's continued interest in reviving a nuclear program.

Iraq's expanding international trade provides growing access to nuclear-related technology and materials and potential access to foreign nuclear expertise. An increase in dual-use procurement activity in recent years may be supporting a reconstituted nuclear weapons program.

- The acquisition of sufficient fissile material is Iraq's principal hurdle in developing a nuclear weapon.

- **Iraq is unlikely to produce indigenously enough weapons-grade material for a deliverable nuclear weapon until the last half of this decade. Baghdad could produce a nuclear weapon within a year if it were able to procure weapons-grade fissile material abroad.**

Baghdad may have acquired uranium enrichment capabilities that could shorten substantially the amount of time necessary to make a nuclear weapon.

Iraq: Declared Nuclear Facilities

Chemical Warfare Program

Iraq has the ability to produce chemical warfare (CW) agents within its chemical industry, although it probably depends on external sources for some precursors. Baghdad is expanding its infrastructure, under cover of civilian industries, that it could use to advance its CW agent production capability. During the 1980s Saddam had a formidable CW capability that he used against Iranians and against Iraq's Kurdish population. Iraqi forces killed or injured more than 20,000 people in multiple attacks, delivering chemical agents (including mustard agent[1] and the nerve agents sarin and tabun[2]) in aerial bombs, 122mm rockets, and artillery shells against both tactical military targets and segments of Iraq's Kurdish population. Before the 1991 Gulf war, Baghdad had a large stockpile of chemical munitions and a robust indigenous production capacity.

Documented Iraqi Use of Chemical Weapons

Date	Area Used	Type of Agent	Approximate Casualties	Target Population
Aug 1983	Hajj Umran	Mustard	fewer than 100	Iranians/Kurds
Oct-Nov 1983	Panjwin	Mustard	3,000	Iranian/Kurds
Feb-Mar 1984	Majnoon Island	Mustard	2,500	Iranians
Mar 1984	al-Basrah	Tabun	50 to 100	Iranians
Mar 1985	Hawizah Marsh	Mustard/Tabun	3,000	Iranians
Feb 1986	al-Faw	Mustard/Tabun	8,000 to 10,000	Iranians
Dec 1986	Umm ar Rasas	Mustard	thousands	Iranians
Apr 1987	al-Basrah	Mustard/Tabun	5,000	Iranians
Oct 1987	Sumar/Mehran	Mustard/nerve agents	3,000	Iranians
Mar 1988	Halabjah	Mustard/nerve agents	hundreds	Iranians/Kurds

---

[1] Mustard is a blister agent that causes medical casualties by blistering or burning exposed skin, eyes, lungs, and mucus membranes within hours of exposure. It is a persistent agent that can remain a hazard for days.

[2] Sarin, cyclosarin, and tabun are G-series nerve agents that can act within seconds of absorption through the skin or inhalation. These agents overstimulate muscles or glands with messages transmitted from nerves, causing convulsions and loss of consciousness. Tabun is persistent and can remain a hazard for days. Sarin and cyclosarin are not persistent and pose more of an inhalation hazard than a skin hazard.

Iraqi 250-gauge chemical bomb.

Iraqi 500-gauge chemical bombs.

Iraqi DB-2 chemical bomb.

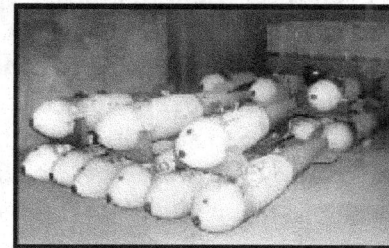

Iraqi R-400 chemical bombs.

Iraqi 155-mm chemical shell.

Iraqi Al Husayn chemical warheads.

122-mm rockets filled with the chemical nerve agent sarin prior to destruction.

Although precise information is lacking, human rights organizations have received plausible accounts from Kurdish villagers of even more Iraqi chemical attacks against civilians in the 1987 to 1988 time frame—with some attacks as late as October 1988—in areas close to the Iranian and Turkish borders.

- UNSCOM supervised the destruction of more than 40,000 chemical munitions, nearly 500,000 liters of chemical agents, 1.8 million liters of chemical precursors, and seven different types of delivery systems, including ballistic missile warheads.

More than 10 years after the Gulf war, gaps in Iraqi accounting and current production capabilities strongly suggest that Iraq maintains a stockpile of chemical agents, probably VX,[3] sarin, cyclosarin,[4] and mustard.

- **Iraq probably has concealed precursors, production equipment, documentation, and other items necessary for continuing its CW effort.** Baghdad never supplied adequate evidence to support its claims that it destroyed all of its CW agents and munitions. Thousands of tons of chemical precursors and tens of thousands of unfilled munitions, including Scud-variant missile warheads, remain unaccounted for.

- UNSCOM discovered a document at Iraqi Air Force headquarters in July 1998 showing that Iraq overstated by at least 6,000 the number of chemical bombs it told the UN it had used during the Iran-Iraq War—bombs that remain are unaccounted for.

- Iraq has not accounted for 15,000 artillery rockets that in the past were its preferred means for delivering nerve agents, nor has it accounted for about 550 artillery shells filled with mustard agent.

- Iraq probably has stocked at least 100 metric tons (MT) and possibly as much as 500 MT of CW agents.

Baghdad continues to rebuild and expand dual-use infrastructure that it could divert quickly to CW production. The best examples are the chlorine and phenol plants at the Fallujah II facility. Both chemicals have legitimate civilian uses but also are raw materials for the synthesis of precursor chemicals used to produce blister and nerve agents. Iraq has three other chlorine plants that have much higher capacity for civilian production; these plants and Iraqi imports are more than sufficient to meet Iraq's civilian

---

[3] VX is a V-series nerve agent that is similar to but more advanced than G-series nerve agents in that it causes the same medical effects but is more toxic and much more persistent. Thus, it poses a far greater skin hazard than G-series agents. VX could be used for long-term contamination of territory.

[4] See footnote 5.

needs for water treatment. Of the 15 million kg of chlorine imported under the UN Oil-for-Food Program since 1997, Baghdad used only 10 million kg and has 5 million kg in stock, suggesting that some domestically produced chlorine has been diverted to such proscribed activities as CW agent production.

- Fallujah II was one of Iraq's principal CW precursor production facilities before the Gulf war. In the last two years the Iraqis have upgraded the facility and brought in new chemical reactor vessels and shipping containers with a large amount of production equipment. They have expanded chlorine output far beyond pre-Gulf war production levels—capabilities that can be diverted quickly to CW production. Iraq is seeking to purchase CW agent precursors and applicable production equipment and is trying to hide the activities of the Fallujah plant.

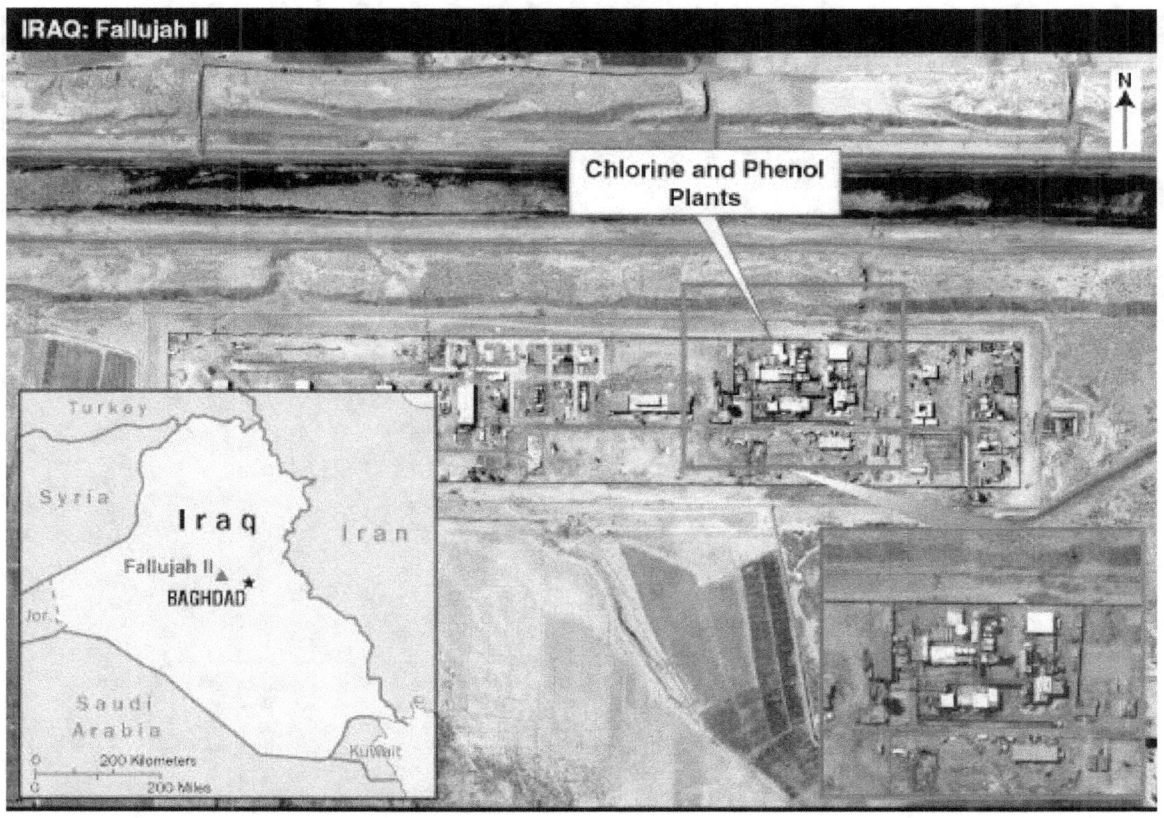

Iraq: CW-Related Production Facilities and Declared Sites of Deployed Alcohol-Filled or Chemical Agent–Filled Munitions During Desert Storm

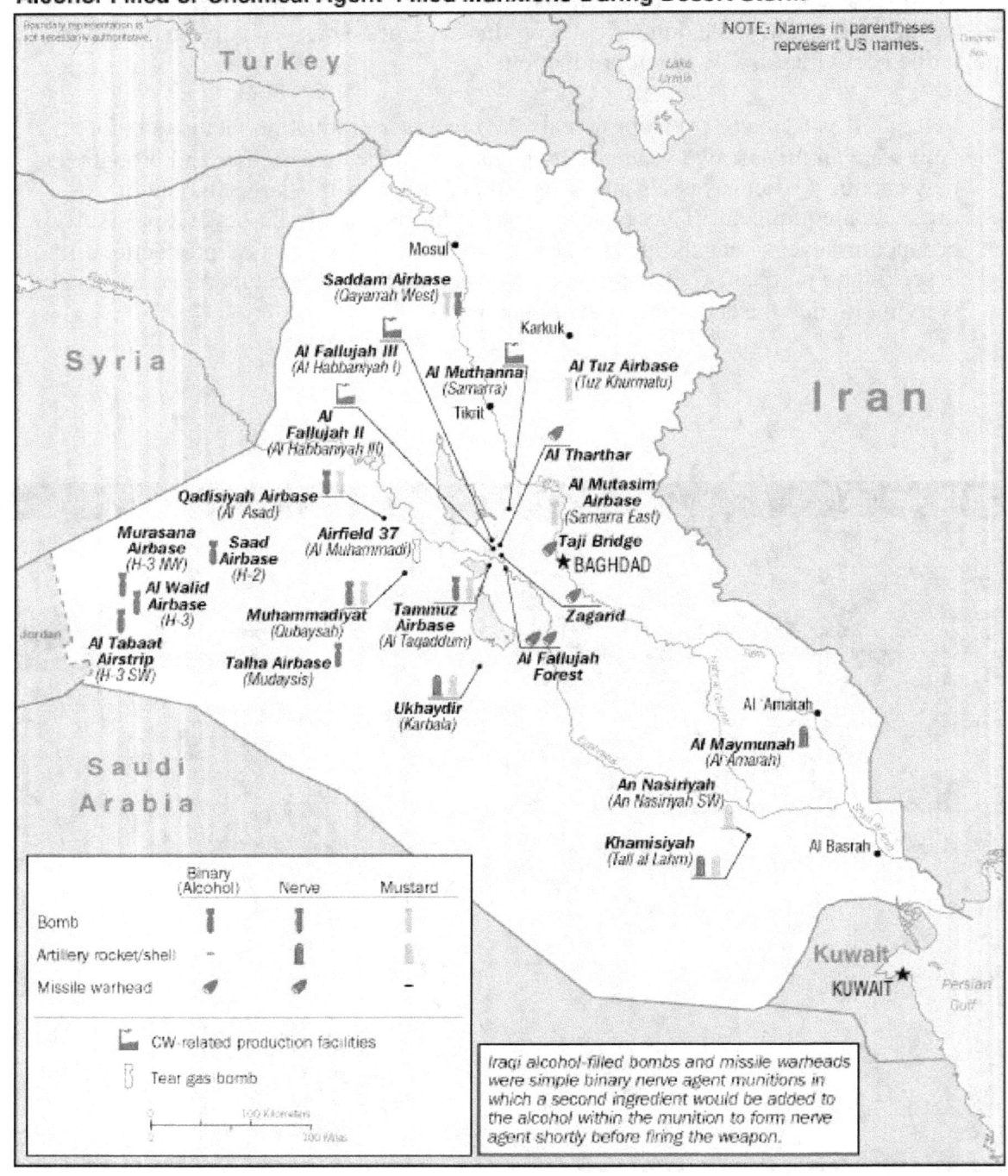

Biological Warfare Program

Iraq has the capability to convert quickly legitimate vaccine and biopesticide plants to biological warfare (BW) production and already may have done so. This capability is particularly troublesome because Iraq has a record of concealing its BW activities and lying about the existence of its offensive BW program.

After four years of claiming that they had conducted only "small-scale, defensive" research, Iraqi officials finally admitted to inspectors in 1995 to production and weaponization of biological agents. The Iraqis admitted this only after being faced with evidence of their procurement of a large volume of growth media and the defection of Husayn Kamil, former director of Iraq's military industries.

Two R-400A bombs in foreground photographed by UNSCOM inspectors at Murasana Airfield near the Al Walid Airbase in late 1991 bear markings indicating they were to be filled with botulinum toxin. Other bombs appear to have markings consistent with binary chemical agent fill. This evidence contradicted Iraq's declarations that it did not deploy BW munitions to operational airbases and that it destroyed all BW bombs in July 1991—declarations that were subsequently retracted in the face of overwhelming evidence to the contrary.

Iraq: Declared BW-Related Sites

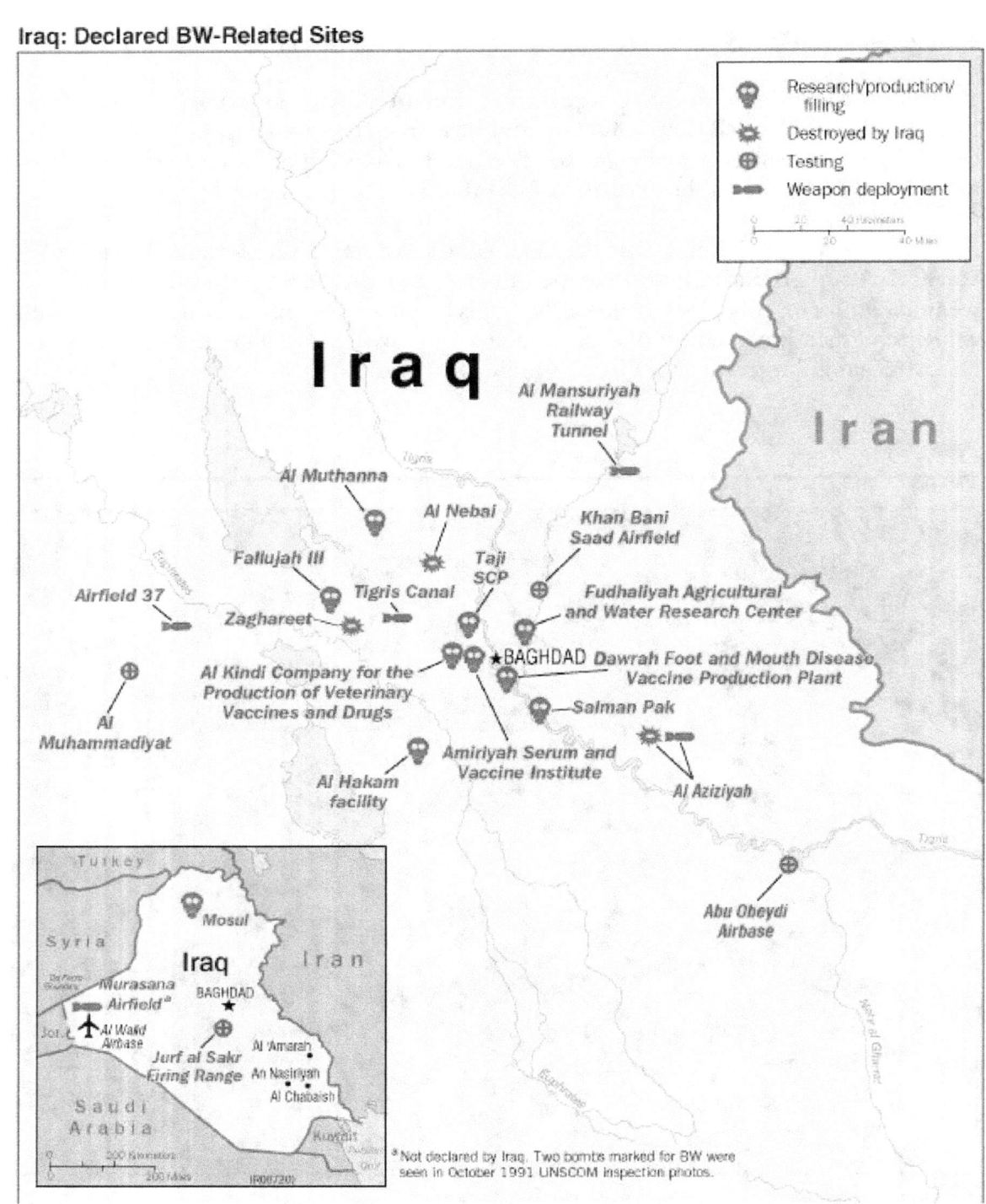

Legend:
- Research/production/filling
- Destroyed by Iraq
- Testing
- Weapon deployment

Al Mansuriyah Railway Tunnel

Al Muthanna

Al Nebai

Khan Bani Saad Airfield

Fallujah III

Taji SCP

Tigris Canal

Fudhaliyah Agricultural and Water Research Center

Airfield 37

Zaghareet

Al Kindi Company for the Production of Veterinary Vaccines and Drugs

★BAGHDAD Dawrah Foot and Mouth Disease Vaccine Production Plant

Al Muhammadiyat

Salman Pak

Amiriyah Serum and Vaccine Institute

Al Hakam facility

Al Aziziyah

Abu Obeydi Airbase

Iraq

Iran

Tigris

Euphrates

Inset map:

Turkey

Syria

Mosul

Iraq

Iran

Murasana Airfield[a]

BAGHDAD

Al Walid Airbase

Jurf al Sakr Firing Range

Al 'Amarah

An Nasiriyah

Al Chabaish

Saudi Arabia

Kuwait

[a] Not declared by Iraq. Two bombs marked for BW were seen in October 1991 UNSCOM inspection photos.

14

Iraqi-Acknowledged Open-Air Testing of Biological Weapons

Location-Date	Agent	Munition
Al Muhammadiyat – Mar 1988	*Bacillus subtilis*[5]	250-gauge bomb (cap. 65 liters)
Al Muhammadiyat – Mar 1988	*Botulinum toxin*	250-gauge bomb (cap. 65 liters)
Al Muhammadiyat – Nov 1989	*Bacillus subtilis*	122mm rocket (cap. 8 liters)
Al Muhammadiyat – Nov 1989	*Botulinum toxin*	122mm rocket (cap. 8 liters)
Al Muhammadiyat – Nov 1989	Aflatoxin	122mm rocket (cap. 8 liters)
Khan Bani Saad – Aug 1988	*Bacillus subtilis*	aerosol generator – Mi-2 helicopter with modified agricultural spray equipment
Al Muhammadiyat – Dec 1989	*Bacillus subtilis*	R-400 bomb (cap. 85 liters)
Al Muhammadiyat – Nov 1989	*Botulinum toxin*	R-400 bomb (cap. 85 liters)
Al Muhammadiyat – Nov 1989	Aflatoxin	R-400 bomb (cap. 85 liters)
Jurf al-Sakr Firing Range – Sep 1989	Ricin	155mm artillery shell (cap. 3 liters)
Abu Obeydi Airfield – Dec 1990	Water	Modified Mirage F1 drop-tank (cap. 2,200 liters)
Abu Obeydi Airfield – Dec 1990	Water/potassium permanganate	Modified Mirage F1 drop-tank (cap. 2,200 liters)
Abu Obeydi Airfield – Jan 1991	Water/glycerine	Modified Mirage F1 drop-tank (cap. 2,200 liters)
Abu Obeydi Airfield – Jan 1991	*Bacillus subtilis*/Glycerine	Modified Mirage F1 drop-tank (cap. 2,200 liters)

- Iraq admitted producing thousands of liters of the BW agents anthrax,[6] botulinum toxin, (which paralyzes respiratory muscles and can be fatal within 24 to 36 hours), and aflatoxin, (a potent carcinogen that can attack the liver, killing years after ingestion), and preparing BW-filled Scud-variant missile warheads, aerial bombs, and aircraft spray tanks before the Gulf war.

Baghdad did not provide persuasive evidence to support its claims that it unilaterally destroyed its BW agents and munitions. **Experts from UNSCOM assessed that Baghdad's declarations vastly understated the production of biological agents and estimated that Iraq actually produced two-to-four times the amount of agent that it acknowledged producing,** including *Bacillus anthracis*—the causative agent of anthrax—and botulinum toxin.

The improvement or expansion of a number of nominally "civilian" facilities that were directly associated with biological weapons indicates that key aspects of Iraq's offensive BW program are active and most elements more advanced and larger than before the 1990-1991 Gulf war.

---

[5] *Bacillus subtilis* is commonly used as a simulant for *B. anthracis*.

[6] An infectious dose of anthrax is about 8,000 spores, or less than one-millionth of a gram in a non immuno-compromised person. Inhalation anthrax historically has been 100 percent fatal within five to seven days, although in recent cases aggressive medical treatment has reduced the fatality rate.

- The al-Dawrah Foot-and-Mouth Disease (FMD) Vaccine Facility is one of two known Biocontainment Level-3—facilities in Iraq with an extensive air handling and filtering system. Iraq admitted that before the Gulf war Al-Dawrah had been a BW agent production facility. UNSCOM attempted to render it useless for BW agent production in 1996 but left some production equipment in place because UNSCOM could not prove it was connected to previous BW work. In 2001, Iraq announced it would begin renovating the plant without UN approval, ostensibly to produce a vaccine to combat an FMD outbreak. In fact, Iraq easily can import all the foot-and-mouth vaccine it needs through the UN.

- The Amiriyah Serum and Vaccine Institute is an ideal cover location for BW research, testing, production, and storage. UN inspectors discovered documents related to BW research at this facility, some showing that BW cultures, agents, and equipment were stored there during the Gulf war. Of particular concern is the plant's new storage capacity, which greatly exceeds Iraq's needs for legitimate medical storage.

- The Fallujah III Castor Oil Production Plant is situated on a large complex with an historical connection to Iraq's CW program. Of immediate BW concern is the

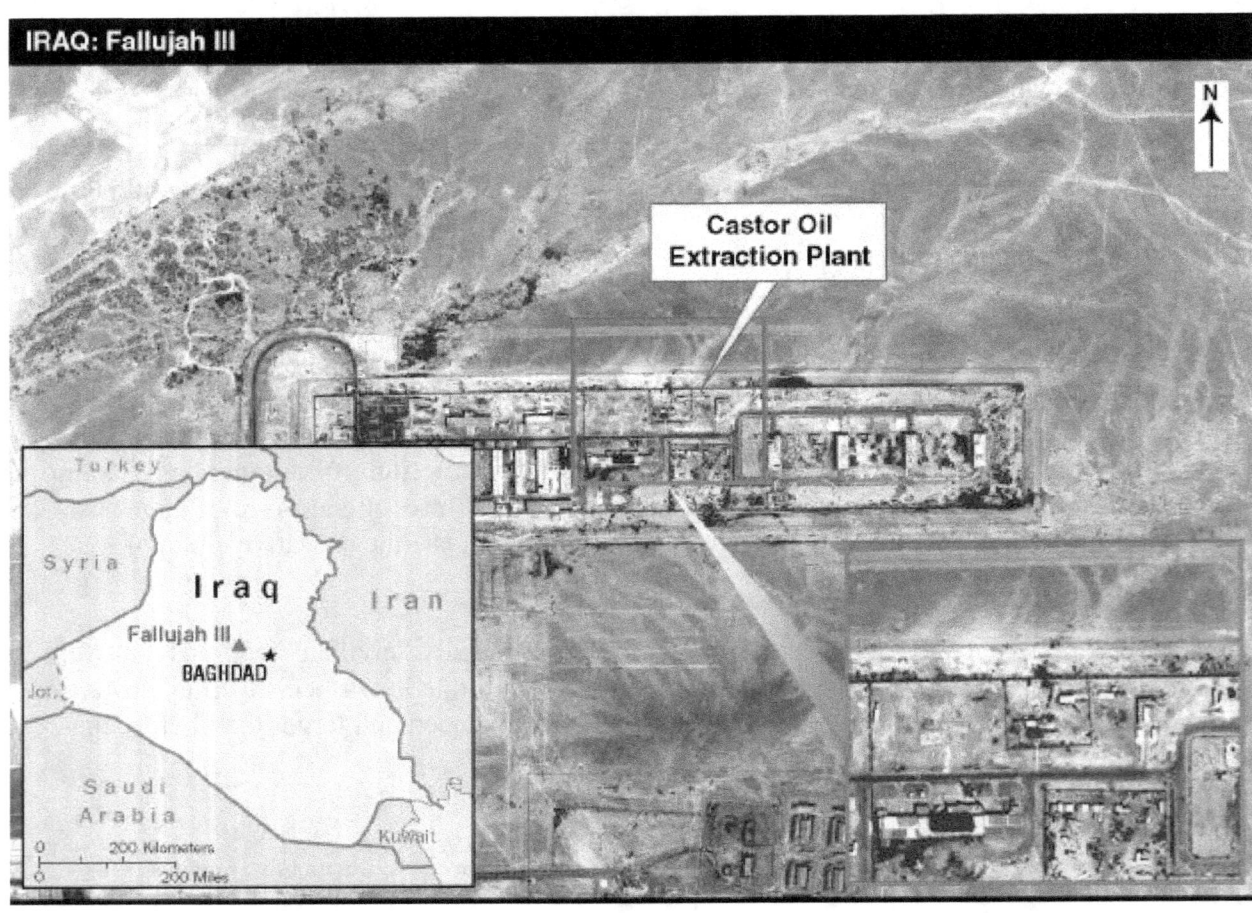

potential production of ricin toxin.[7] Castor bean pulp, left over from castor oil production, can be used to extract ricin toxin. Iraq admitted to UNSCOM that it manufactured ricin and field-tested it in artillery shells before the Gulf war. Iraq operated this plant for legitimate purposes under UNSCOM scrutiny before 1998 when UN inspectors left the country. Since 1999, Iraq has rebuilt major structures destroyed during Operation Desert Fox. Iraqi officials claim they are making castor oil for brake fluid, but verifying such claims without UN inspections is impossible.

In addition to questions about activity at known facilities, **there are compelling reasons to be concerned about BW activity at other sites and in mobile production units and laboratories.** Baghdad has pursued a mobile BW research and production capability to better conceal its program.

- UNSCOM uncovered a document on Iraqi Military Industrial Commission letterhead indicating that Iraq was interested in developing mobile fermentation units, and an Iraqi scientist admitted to UN inspectors that Iraq was trying to move in the direction of mobile BW production.

- Iraq has now established large-scale, redundant, and concealed BW agent production capabilities based on mobile BW facilities.

Ballistic Missile Program

Iraq has developed a ballistic missile capability that exceeds the 150km range limitation established under UNSCR 687. During the 1980s, Iraq purchased 819 Scud B missiles from the USSR. Hundreds of these 300km range missiles were used to attack Iranian cities during the Iran-Iraq War. Beginning in 1987, Iraq converted many of these Soviet Scuds into extended-range variants, some of which were fired at Tehran; some were launched during the Gulf war, and others remained in Iraq's inventory at war's end. Iraq admitted filling at least 75 of its Scud warheads with chemical or biological agents and deployed these weapons for use against Coalition forces and regional opponents, including Israel in 1991.

Most of the approximately 90 Scud-type missiles Saddam fired at Israel, Saudi Arabia, and Bahrain during the Gulf war were al-Husayn variants that the Iraqis modified by lengthening the airframe and increasing fuel capacity, extending the range to 650 km.

Baghdad was developing other longer-range missiles based on Scud technology, including the 900km al-Abbas. Iraq was designing follow-on multi-stage and clustered medium-range ballistic missile (MRBM) concepts with intended ranges up to 3,000 km. Iraq also had a program to develop a two-stage missile, called the Badr-2000, using solid-propellants with an estimated range of 750 to 1,000 km.

---

[7] Ricin can cause multiple organ failure within one or two days after inhalation.

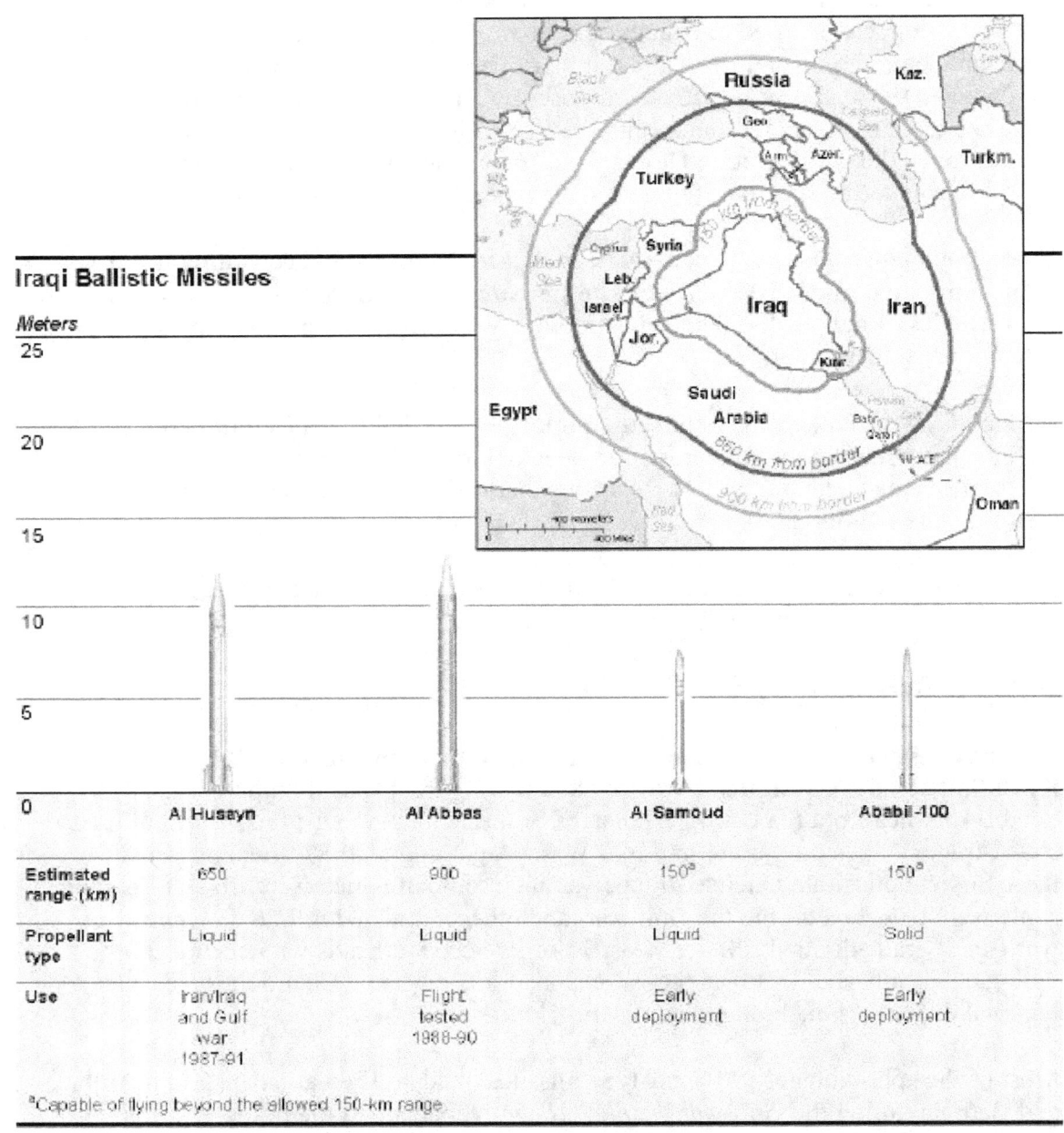

Iraqi Ballistic Missiles

	Al Husayn	Al Abbas	Al Samoud	Ababil-100
Estimated range (km)	650	900	150[a]	150[a]
Propellant type	Liquid	Liquid	Liquid	Solid
Use	Iran/Iraq and Gulf war 1987-91	Flight tested 1988-90	Early deployment	Early deployment

[a]Capable of flying beyond the allowed 150-km range.

- Iraq never fully accounted for its existing missile programs. Discrepancies in Baghdad's declarations suggest that Iraq retains a small force of extended-range Scud-type missiles and an undetermined number of launchers and warheads. Further, Iraq never explained the disposition of advanced missile components, such as guidance and control systems, that it could not produce on its own and that would be critical to developmental programs.

Iraq continues to work on UN-authorized short-range ballistic missiles (SRBMs)—those with a range no greater than 150 km—that help develop the expertise and infrastructure needed to produce longer-range missile systems. The al-Samoud liquid propellant SRBM and the Ababil-100 solid propellant SRBM, however, are capable of flying beyond the allowed 150km range. Both missiles have been tested aggressively and are in early deployment. Other evidence strongly suggests Iraq is modifying missile testing and production facilities to produce even longer-range missiles.

- The Al-Rafah-North Liquid Propellant Engine Research, Development, Testing, and Evaluation (RDT&E) Facility is Iraq's principal site for the static testing of liquid propellant missile engines. Baghdad has been building a new test stand there that is larger than the test stand associated with al-Samoud engine testing and the defunct Scud engine test stand. The only plausible explanation for this test facility is that Iraq intends to test engines for longer-range missiles prohibited under UNSCR 687.

SA-2 (Al Samoud) Engine Test

Iraq conducted static tests of the SA-2 SAM sustainer engine to support development of the Al Samoud SRBM. This test stand is capable of testing engines for Iraq's UN-authorized liquid-propellant ballistic and anti-ship cruise missiles. The new test stand at Al-Rafah is larger than both this test stand and the defunct Scud engine test stand, indicating Iraqi intentions to test engines for longer-range missiles.

Iraq: Ballistic-Missile-Related Facilities

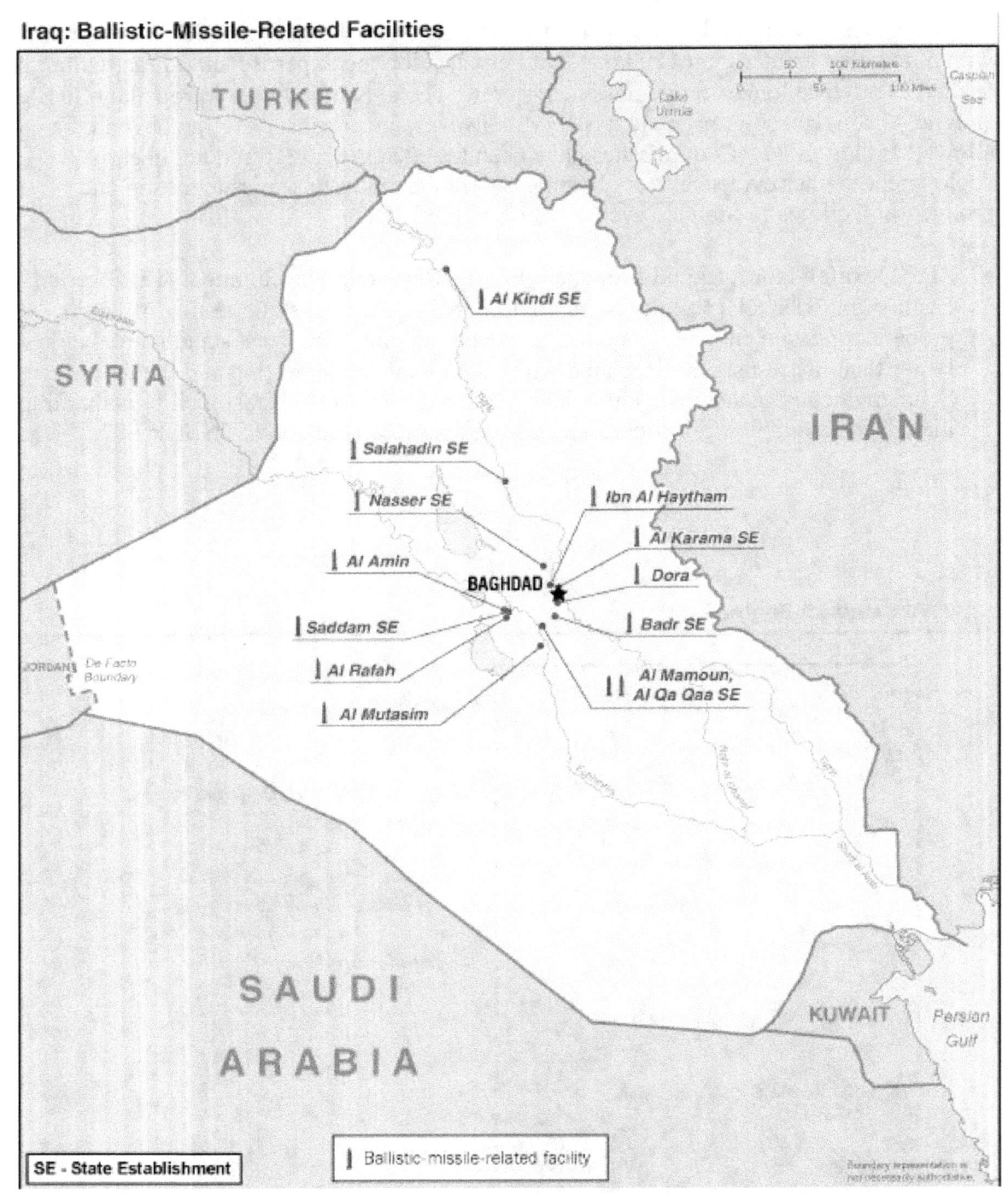

IRAQ: Al Mamoun Solid-Propellant Production Plant

Reconstructed Production Buildings
Earthern Berms

- The Al-Mutasim Solid Rocket Motor and Test Facility, previously associated with Iraq's Badr-2000 solid-propellant missile program, has been rebuilt and expanded in recent years. The al-Mutasim site supports solid-propellant motor assembly, rework, and testing for the UN-authorized Ababil-100, but the size of certain facilities there, particularly those newly constructed between the assembly rework and static test areas, suggests that Baghdad is preparing to develop systems that are prohibited by the UN.

- At the Al-Mamoun Solid Rocket Motor Production Plant and RDT&E Facility, the Iraqis, since the December 1998 departure of inspectors, have rebuilt structures damaged during the Gulf war and dismantled by UNSCOM that originally were built to manufacture solid propellant motors for the Badr-2000 program. They also have built a new building and are reconstructing other buildings originally designed to fill large Badr-2000 motor casings with solid propellant.

- Also at al-Mamoun, the Iraqis have rebuilt two structures used to "mix" solid propellant for the Badr-2000 missile. The new buildings—about as large as the original ones—are ideally suited to house large, UN-prohibited mixers. In fact, the only logical explanation for the size and configuration of these mixing buildings is that Iraq intends to develop longer-range, prohibited missiles.

Iraq has managed to rebuild and expand its missile development infrastructure under sanctions. Iraqi intermediaries have sought production technology, machine tools, and raw materials in violation of the arms embargo.

- The Iraqis have completed a new ammonium perchlorate production plant at Mamoun that supports Iraq's solid propellant missile program. Ammonium perchlorate is a common oxidizer used in solid propellant missile motors. Baghdad would not have been able to complete this facility without help from abroad.

- In August 1995, Iraq was caught trying to acquire sensitive ballistic missile guidance components, including gyroscopes originally used in Russian strategic nuclear SLBMs, demonstrating that Baghdad has been pursuing proscribed, advanced, long-range missile technology for some time. Iraqi officials admitted that, despite international prohibitions, they had received a similar shipment earlier that year.

Unmanned Aerial Vehicle Program and Other Aircraft

Iraq is continuing to develop other platforms which most analysts believe probably are intended for delivering biological warfare agents. Immediately before the Gulf war, Baghdad attempted to convert a MiG-21 into an unmanned aerial vehicle (UAV) to carry spray tanks capable of dispensing chemical or biological agents. UNSCOM assessed that the program to develop the spray system was successful, but the conversion of the MiG-21 was not. More recently, Baghdad has attempted to convert some of its L-29 jet trainer aircraft into UAVs that can be fitted with chemical and biological warfare (CBW) spray tanks, most likely a continuation of previous efforts with the MiG-21. Although much less sophisticated than ballistic missiles as a delivery platform, an aircraft—manned or unmanned—is the most efficient way to disseminate chemical and biological weapons over a large, distant area.

- Iraq already has produced modified drop-tanks that can disperse biological or chemical agents effectively. Before the Gulf war, the Iraqis successfully experimented with aircraft-mounted spray tanks capable of releasing up to 2,000 liters of an anthrax simulant over a target area. Iraq also has modified commercial crop sprayers successfully and tested them with an anthrax simulant delivered by helicopters.

- Baghdad has a history of experimenting with a variety of unmanned platforms. Iraq's use of newer, more capable airframes would increase range and payload, while smaller platforms might be harder to detect and therefore more survivable. This capability represents a serious threat to Iraq's neighbors and to international military forces in the region.

- Iraq used tactical fighter aircraft and helicopters to deliver chemical agents, loaded in bombs and rockets, during the Iran-Iraq War. Baghdad probably is considering again using manned aircraft as delivery platforms depending on the operational scenario.

Procurement in Support of WMD Programs

Iraq has been able to import dual-use, WMD-relevant equipment and material through procurements both within and outside the UN sanctions regime. **Baghdad diverts some of the $10 billion worth of goods now entering Iraq every year for humanitarian needs to support the military and WMD programs instead.** Iraq's growing ability to sell oil illicitly increases Baghdad's capabilities to finance its WMD programs. Over the last four years Baghdad's earnings from illicit oil sales have more than quadrupled to about $3 billion this year.

Test of dissemination of BW agents from a modified drop tank carried by a Mirage F1. The drop tank was filled with 1000 liters of slurry Bacillus subtilis, a simulant for B. anthracis, and disseminated over Abu Obeydi Airbase in January 1991. The photo is from a videotape provided by Iraq to UNSCOM.

- UN monitors at Iraq's borders do not inspect the cargo—worth hundreds of millions of dollars—that enters Iraq every year outside of the Oil-for-Food Program; some of these goods clearly support Iraq's military and WMD programs. For example, Baghdad imports fiber-optic communication systems outside of UN auspices to support the Iraqi military.

- Iraq imports goods using planes, trains, trucks, and ships without any type of international inspections—in violation of UN Security Council resolutions.

Even within the UN-authorized Oil-for-Food Program, Iraq does not hide that it wants to purchase military and WMD-related goods. For example, **Baghdad diverted UN-approved trucks for military purposes and construction equipment to rehabilitate WMD-affiliated facilities, even though these items were approved only to help the civilian population.**

- Iraq has been able to repair modern industrial machine tools that previously supported production of WMD or missile components and has imported additional tools that it may use to reconstitute Baghdad's unconventional weapons arsenal.

- On several occasions, Iraq has asked to purchase goods—such as neutron generators and servo valves—that the UN Monitoring, Verification, and Inspection Commission (UNMOVIC) views as linchpins for prohibited Iraqi programs; alternative, non-dual-use items would serve the civilian purpose purportedly intended for this equipment.

UNMOVIC began screening contracts pursuant to UNSCR 1284 in December 1999 and since has identified more than 100 contracts containing dual-use items as defined in UNSCR 1051 that can be diverted into WMD programs. UNMOVIC also has requested that suppliers provide technical information on hundreds of other goods because of concerns about potential misuse of dual-use equipment. In many cases, Iraq has requested technology that clearly exceeds requirements for the stated commercial end-use when it easily could substitute items that could not be used for WMD.

- On some UN contracts, Baghdad claimed that the requested goods are designed to rehabilitate facilities—such as the Al Qa'im phosphate plant and Fallujah—that in the past were used to support both industrial and WMD programs.